8 Tips to Understand the Opposite Sex

by

DR. GILDA CARLE

Published in New York by
InterChange Communications Training, Inc.

ISBN-13: 978-1-881829-12-6

Library of Congress Control Number: 2015904242

Printed in the United States

For more information visit
www.DrGilda.com

ACKNOWLEDGMENTS

Thank you to all who have so generously contributed
your true stories to help others who are reading this
book. Without your giving, there would be less
healthful living!
--Dr. Gilda

<u>Gilda-Gram®</u>
What seem like *relationship* issues may only be
communication meltdowns—
and these can be fixed!

CONTENTS

INTRODUCTION

TWO SEPARATE CULTURES

Men and women are actually two separate "cultures" that communicate in their own unique way. As a society in general, we listen poorly to each other, with the average listener processing only 25 percent of what he hears—and remembering only 10 percent! So imagine how much more confusing messages become when men speak one way and women speak another.

Women often complain that their men are not sensitive, attentive, caring, or loving enough. And men say they can't fathom what's wrong with their women for talking so much, why women analyze everything men say and do, and why they're never satisfied. What's really going on, and most importantly, how can we fix it so we can sustain our relationships?

Another issue is that after men cozily settle into their relationships, they often treat their women like their pal, rather than like the fictitious princess women would like to be. Consequently, both sexes beef that the spark has dimmed, and their formerly hot romance has turned to ice. *Duh!*

Here's a news flash for both genders:

If we interpret our differences as *challenges*, not *roadblocks*, we'll be able to "decode" what our partners really mean. Then, when we understand each other's languages, we can discuss our differences, actually enjoy them, and even humor each other about them.

The following pages explain 8 Tips to Understand the Opposite Sex. These eight tips will help you re-assess what's at the heart of your communication "issues." Master these tips—and let them become your guide to stronger and more sustainable love.

TIP #1

DECODE YOUR OWN TALK

As the self-appointed "relationship police," women are forever trying to figure out what their men mean by their talk and behavior. They spend countless hours huddled with their girlfriends dissecting situations and conversations that occurred. With all this discussion, one would think women would have the key to gender translations. No such luck! They're still in the dark.

Before investing endless effort in trying to unravel *your partner's* message, consider exactly what it is that *you're* trying to get across. When you figure that out, you'll be better able to understand your honey's response, and know how to interpret it.

Hi, Dr. Gilda,
    I've been in an on-again-off-again relationship with my ex-husband for 5 years. We've been married and divorced, we have a child, and we've lived together through job terminations and dying relatives. Somehow, we're still together, although now we live apart. I believe I have taken good care of myself. I have a house of my own (which I bought myself), plenty of savings, a beautiful daughter, a college

degree, and a career I worked hard for. I literally struggled to make myself a prize for the right man--for him.

When I first met my husband, we had a deep friendship that developed into love. He stayed with me through my college years, and then married me when I returned home. He has given me my strength. Our married life developed so rapidly, I wonder where the time went.

We don't hug anymore, we hardly kiss, and he rarely listens to what I say. We don't go to dinner or even "date" as we used to. Stuck in a rut, I feel I have lost his love and respect, and I am constantly fighting to win it back. Maybe it's my insecurity talking.

Since our divorce, Jeff has done a complete turnaround. He's gone from insecure to secure, and irresponsible to responsible. Along the way, our "love" changed and it saddens me. I feel like I have lost someone. When he becomes cold, I respond to him in the same way. This freeze-out can go on for days.

Usually, it is a bad fight that warms us again to each other. But our reconciliation only lasts a short time. Am I fighting for nothing?
Patty

Like most women, Patty feels totally responsible for the downward spiral her marriage has taken. At the beginning, she worked hard to snag her husband, and now she intends to work just as hard to keep him. Before we can identify what is wrong in her relationship, however, we must determine what Patty is really saying.

Dear Patty,

What happened to your relationship is what typically occurs in many marriages: two people settle into their routines, and quickly relinquish the romance that brought them together. While your marriage was developing, your husband grew emotionally, and you grew intellectually and professionally. However, you still remained "insecure" in the union. Your email communicates volumes more than you realize. Let's examine your specific words.

1) You said, "When I first met my husband . . . he stayed with me through my college years, and then married me when I returned home." Your words suggest you believe your husband practically did you a favor by waiting for you to return from college.

Gilda-Gram®
A relationship of mutual power says, "We stayed together," not "He stayed with me."

To support my argument, look at the words you use to describe how your marriage came about. You say,

"He married me," instead of "we got married." So, from the very start, you placed yourself in the subordinate position, making him the dominant force. In real life, a woman who places a man on a pedestal will find the distance between them is very great, and eventually that distance will erode the union.

<u>Gilda-Gram®</u>
Putting your man on a pedestal leaves you way down below.

No relationship can survive when one partner looks down on the other. That sets up a parent/child kind of involvement, rather than a healthy partnership of equals. A parent/child relationship may seem almost "cute" at first, but eventually, most men prefer to relate to their woman on their own level. Also, in time, when a woman grows up and wishes to relinquish the child role, she may resent being treated in the old childish way.

2) You said, "I literally struggled to make myself a prize for the right man—for him." Love should never be a game of "Hunter Takes All." You deliberately enhanced your image NOT FOR YOURSELF, but so your husband would pick you as his life's mate.

Self-improvement is great, but your goal was not based on your own internal drive toward a better you.

You manipulatively set out to become a trophy that your man could not resist. It worked for a while—as it often does. But eventually, the lure of a shiny souvenir only lasts for so long. Now your husband obviously recognizes your desperation and insecurity, and that's never a turn-on to any man.

3) You said, "Since our divorce, Jeff has done a complete turnaround. He's gone from insecure to secure, and irresponsible to responsible. Along the way, our 'love' changed and it saddens me." Your husband has apparently done a great deal of work on himself after the two of you split, which shows the divorce was good for at least one of you.

In contrast to the outer improvements you made, you also got financial security, a home of your own, and a successful career. Meanwhile, Jeff became an emotional grown-up, thereby enhancing his inner strength. Sure, when he was young and insecure, "possessing" a radiant keepsake of a wife was almost a mandate for him to feel better about himself. But since he's changed, he no longer needs to bolster a weak self-image. Now he evidently prefers an adult as a partner.

Gilda-Gram®
People are attracted to people like themselves.

You've been trying to get your husband to come back to you. But you are finding that the old manipulative tools you used in the past no longer work; Jeff has become his own person, too strong to allow superficial traits to seduce him.

You know your "love" is off base because you put the word in quotes. You can begin healing by admitting you manufactured the emotion specifically to become part of a pair, rather than to enhance your own self-worth.

4) You said, "He has given me my strength." In every healthy marriage, partners naturally depend on support from one another, inviting one person's depletion to draw from the other's supply source. But a spouse in a subordinate role takes more than she gives. This leaves her mate exhausted and drained. In time, her mate begins to resent being sucked dry from a union that was supposed to be mutually reassuring. While your husband had once been insecure and irresponsible, his own neediness for adoration kept him with you. But after he grew, he wanted a more meaningful, two-way partnership.

5) Finally, you admit, "Usually it is a bad fight that warms us again to each other." While you are fighting, your husband gets a glimpse of a woman with her own thoughts and feelings, not one freeze-dried specifically to snag a man. This is a turn-on for him.

Gilda-Gram®
**Independent women are aphrodisiacs
to grown-up men.**

*You've unlocked the door to getting back Jeff's
attention. However, since you discovered that anger has
become your love potion, be careful not to incite riot to
get affection. It will no longer work.*

Gilda-Gram®
**Anger may be a precursor to passion, but
that won't make it the foundation for love.**

*Do you want a re-marriage based on your knack
for ticking each other off? If you get into that sorry
state, both of you will be so spent from arguing that
you'll barely be able to meet your other life's goals.*

*When you are speaking to Jeff—or anyone, for
that matter—carefully decode your language as we have
done here. The words we all use provide the key to the
way others respond. Instead of blaming Jeff for
withdrawing, change your approach, and see how much
more positively he responds. That's your best hope for a
renewed marriage, if you have a shot at it at this point.
Dr. Gilda*

I'm sure Patty had no idea that her words "said" as much as they did. In subsequent correspondence, I recommended that instead of seeing a couples' therapist, Patty find a counselor who would work with her individually to grow her personal self-worth. I also recommended she read my book, "I'm Worth Loving! Here's Why."

Since Patty was successful at other things, she already had a track record of knowing how to work hard for what she wants. Whether Jeff continues to be in her life or not is less important now than Patty's need to understand her motives and language, and to channel positive messages so they're well received.

TIP #2

TEST YOUR LISTENER'S READINESS

At times, we're so anxious to share personal information, we ignore whether our listener is ready and available to process it. Lauren had just begun a live-in arrangement with her boyfriend of three years, Paul. Paul worked late Thursday night and by the time he got home, Lauren was fast asleep. Not to wake her, he tiptoed into bed, and soon fell asleep himself.

The next morning, when they awoke, the two of them quietly and sleepily shared breakfast. All at once, amid the quietness, Lauren launched into her description of the day before, the day she had missed talking about with Paul. She described the people at her job, she listed who was jockeying for a newly posted position, and she visualized how she intended to introduce herself to her new clients of the day.

Paul looked on, bleary-eyed. But Lauren continued chattering about people and things relatively foreign to her boyfriend. Suddenly, as diplomatically as he could, he commented, "Honey, you are awfully chatty this morning." What Paul really meant was, "Damn, woman! It's too early for this. Will you shut up, already?"

Lauren was so immersed in her dialogue, she totally missed her boyfriend's cue to shelve it for another time, when he was more ready to listen. Instead, her mouth kept going.

This couple had just begun what they hoped would evolve into a life-long future. Both were still in the "honeymoon" stage of getting to know how to co-habit. To keep the peace, Paul already fell into the routine of what a lot of men do. Of course, the cartoon caricature of how men don't listen shows a guy burying his face in his newspaper as his woman yaps on, into deaf ears. Its truth makes for good humor, but it also underscores one of the top complaints women have about their men: they don't listen.

Not wanting to get into an argument, and not wanting to tell Lauren directly to put a lid on it, Paul did what most men in this situation do: he tuned Lauren out. This behavior may be a fine coping mechanism to use occasionally, especially when a relationship is new, but when the tune-out continues over the course of years, a couple's closeness disintegrates.

Our two genders use talk in different ways, and

for different reasons. Talk for women is a way of getting closer. Talk for men is a means of exchanging information. In her classic book, "You Just Don't Understand: Women and Men in Conversation," Deborah Tannen aptly calls female talk, "rapport talk," and male talk, "report talk."

Without going out on a limb and being mushy in the morning, Lauren's spewing was a result of her having missed her boyfriend's presence the day before. Going on endlessly about her work was her way of letting Paul know her loving feelings for him, without actually saying them in words. But how was he to know?

Lauren did not bother to assess whether he was ready to be receptive. Ignoring the cue that Paul was barely awake, Lauren displayed poor observation skills in her self-centered quest for attention and affection.

In my book, "Don't Bet on the Prince! How to Have the Man You Want by Betting on Yourself," I recommend three listening skills to insure love's longevity:

1. Consider your partner's readiness to hear what you are offering.
2. Observe your listener's behavior while you talk, so you can adjust your message accordingly.

3.   Invite feedback so you know that what
       you're saying is what he's hearing.

Acknowledging your listener's readiness for your information is not only a considerate gesture, but also a matter of respect and love.

Having known Paul for a few years before living with him, Lauren was well versed in his listening style. But now that they were cohabiting, she needed to look beyond her own immediate needs that worked for her while single, and recognize that this guy's needs count, too. When a couple begins to live together, changes must be made. They can't behave as they did while they were single, believing it's merely a matter of moving their furniture under one roof.

Unfortunately, many communicators just want to get their message out, regardless of whether the timing is right. If you are one of these people, consider this:

Gilda-Gram®

**A *child* wants immediate gratification.
An *adult* is willing to wait.**

No grownup wants to be accused of acting like a child. Communication differences between the sexes are already difficult, but whoever your listener is, remember that:

Gilda-Gram®

As with most things in life, timing is everything.

Your listener's receptivity is usually a matter of timing. If you are caring enough to find the optimal time of your listener, you'll get the attention—and reception—you seek.

TIP #3

LIMIT YOUR DETAILS

Since men want a simple report, while women want fluffy rapport, each sex must appreciate the fact that:

Gilda-Gram®
Men talk deals; women talk details.

Because this often eludes even the most savvy communicators, men are constantly accusing women of talking too much—even though research finds that is it *men* that actually talk *more* than women! On the other hand, while women keep blabbing, they forever blame men for being closed down!!

Of course, these are generalizations. There's a guy I dated who wouldn't stop telling me every single detail of every single story he unfolded. Perhaps I'm just used to the male bottom-line model, or perhaps I was just turned off to this guy, but whatever it was, I didn't want to continue seeing him. Yet, a complaint I often had with a lot of the men I dated was that they were too withholding and closed down. So I ended up fitting the same female stereotype I've been outlining here: While we women criticize guys for their refusal to share and become open books, we really can't stand it when a guy is overly forthcoming. This behavior makes guys crazy, and it surely makes us seem as though we suffer from a bipolar disorder!!

Because of the sweeping stereotype that men are more knowledgeable than women, most women feel more secure when they pad their comments with extra words and information to prove their own self- worth. I especially see women's desire for acceptance when I ask college and graduate students to submit papers. While male students are happy to give me unedited and half-completed versions of their work, women would rather get a late grade than be judged on a paper with undotted i's and uncrossed t's. That is because, above and beyond anything else, the motive for women is to be liked.

In "Don't Bet on the Prince!," I name most women "Toastmasters" in their desire for approval, while I call most men "Taskmasters" in their plight to accomplish their task, regardless of their likeability. Of course, these are again stereotypes. But in reality, to succeed in life and love, both genders should display a balance of both traits. And that requires each of us to stretch our natural tendencies.

One of the traits Toastmaster women have in abundance is talking a subject to death. This drives men crazy, since they prefer to hear their information short and to the point. So the question for women is, "How much talk is too much talk?"

Dear Dr. Gilda,

I am a 25-year-old woman married for 5 months. The problem is that I can't get my husband to open up to me. He will only tell me bits and pieces of things going on in his life. On the other hand, I tell him everything.

At first, because of his reluctance to share, I thought he was cheating. Each time I accused him of this, we'd get into a tremendous argument, and I'd run off in tears. He assures me he loves me, and that there's nobody else.

I have gotten past my fears that he's involved with someone else, and I am trying a new tact. He is in the Navy. When he is here, I sit him down and explain what I want him to do in the house. He says okay, but then he never follows through. So this is not working either.

While he was in boot camp, we talked on the phone for hours, twice a day. Now that we are married and living together, we go for long periods without even saying a word. What can I do?
Crystal

Miscommunication can certainly lead to

misjudgment. Crystal's husband was verbally shut down. Instead of interpreting this as a function of male talk, like many women, Crystal personalized it to mean he not only didn't love her, but that he had another woman on the side.

When she accused him and confronted him, her husband's reaction proved that he was still alive, breathing, and *in love*. As crazy as it may seem, subconsciously, Crystal believed it was in her best interests to continue her badgering, because that was the only time she was able to get hubby to hear her. However, too much arguing wears any couple out.

Dear Crystal,
  In part, you can attribute your insecurity in your marriage to the differences in the way men and women express their feelings. During your courtship, you and your husband spoke endlessly. That proves he's a capable communicator. But like many men, as soon as he settled into a stable marriage, he withdrew into coach-potato comfort.

  Most men believe that to "get the girl," they must initially go outside their comfort zone and become romantic and mushy. They can't wait to secure permanent bonding, so they can return to a more comfortable quiet and introspective existence.

  While women unconsciously believe, "If he talks to me, he loves me," men assess their role differently.

Gilda-Gram®

Men reason that JUST BEING with their lady proves they care.

Crystal, understand that in your husband's mind, his continuing to return home "says" he loves you. As you try to bolster your relationship with talk, you are finding that your detailed conversations are not getting him to talk more. In fact, they are having the opposite effect, unless you interrogate him with questions about the relationship's status. When you do this, he is thrown into worry about the security of the cushy comfort he has come to enjoy.

Your provocations will not assure his continued comfort. Nor will your demanding he do chores around the house. Your man is traveling so much that when he returns home, he wants to relax in a place where he doesn't have to follow orders. A wife giving her husband orders demeans his masculinity.

Your approaches have all been off base. Instead of the tactics you have been trying, to get your husband to open up: 1) Make your home a safe environment for him, so he doesn't feel judged; 2) Let him trust that you won't be badgering him, like his superior officer at sea. Finally, 3) Let him know you value what he says by responding with approval.

Gilda-Gram®

Men open up when they feel safe, trusted, and valued.

Despite what this Gilda-Gram® says, I do need to caution women here. If you believe you've done and said everything you could to provide an open and trusting environment for your man to share his most inner thoughts, and he is still withholding, DON'T BLAME YOURSELF. Your guy may have been raised in a generally untrusting environment, and no matter what you do, he'll may still be reluctant to display what he feels is his underbelly.

Yet, don't think you learned these new skills for naught. If you stay with this dude, you'll be more ready to accept him as he is, without trying to change him, while secretly seething because he's not different. If you leave, you'll always have these skills to apply in your next relationship.

Chrystal, show your husband how comfortable your home can be. When he feels secure that you won't be nagging him or assigning him one chore after another, he will feel comfortable enough to return to the kinds of conversations you had before you were married.

If a man was once forthcoming, with your encouragement, he can eventually return to those behaviors. But in order for this to occur, your obvious

support of your guy is crucial.
Dr. Gilda

Women must acknowledge that men process deals instead of details, and that they prefer to hear basic information first, in a few sentences. After women have set up this kind of communication format, they can ask their man if he wants to hear more. This approach proves that you're respectful of your guy's listening style. After his astonishment about how much you are suddenly appreciating him, he will probably ask you much more about what you have to say. But since you now know the secret, it's got to start with you.

One Last Caveat: A major problem arises when women try to get their men to listen the way their girlfriends do. If that's your situation, get over it! *This is another reason never to give up your friends after you become involved with a man.* Both genders offer us different kinds of supportive emotions. To be happy and in balance, we all need both kinds of interactions.

TIP #4

TRUST YOUR GUT TO GUIDE YOU

Research points to women's intuition as an asset in their communications. How often do we "feel" the "truth," yet let it escape because we don't trust our own feelings? See if the "Female Interpretation" of the man's behavior below rings true for you.

The Meeting

Leila was attending a large, glamorous political event in New York City. People were dressed in their finest and slinkiest duds, and the buzz was enormous. After the dinner and show, remaining guests went for nightcaps at a small rooftop party. It was there that, as the song goes, "from across a crowded room," Leila exchanged glances with a tall, rugged man in a black tuxedo. Amid the throngs of people, they were finally pushed together. His name was Barry and he was a television reporter from upstate New York, covering the festivities. After a half hour of political banter, they exchanged business cards, said goodnight, and went their separate ways. That was Saturday night.

The Chase—Or Was It a Limp?

Monday evening of the next week, Barry called Leila. He said he would be visiting New York City again in two weeks on business, and asked if she would like to get together. He suggested either lunch or dinner. To a woman, "lunch" means casual interest, whereas "dinner" suggests something more. Leila was smitten with this handsome stranger, so of course, she chose dinner.

The pair spent 45 minutes on the phone discussing politics in the city. "Strange," thought Leila. "He never once revealed anything about his personal life. He didn't say whether he had been married, if he has kids, or what he likes. Nor did he ask about me." But she decided she would let him take the lead, and see where it went.

They exchanged email addresses, and promised to communicate during the two-week span they would be apart. Customarily, most guys try to get to know a woman somewhat before seeing her. So Leila assumed Barry would call or text to have a few conversations before they went on their date.

A few days after they spoke, she received an email from him: "Hello Leila, Great web site you have. Did you see my station's special piece today about Ebola?" The email went on for four paragraphs about the coverage, and then on to political events in New York. In the very last sentence, he wrote, "As I said on the phone, I'm planning to be in the city on the weekend of the 28th. Which do you prefer—lunch or dinner? Best regards, Barry."

Female Interpretation: "He's asking the same question again?? Another guy who doesn't listen!"

But deciding not to jump to critical conclusions, Leila sent back a sweet note re-stating her preference for dinner. Two days later, she received a second email: "Hi, Leila, Thanks for your reply . . . I'm getting back to you from my home, rather than at work. Here's another piece about the conversation we had on Saturday night when we met." He attached information about a political fiasco occurring that week in New York. Since it was St. Patrick's Day, he signed it, "Erin go bragh, Barry."

A few days had passed when Leila got this: "Hi, Leila, I just hatched an idea for a story we could run on this evening's news. What do you think?" He described his creative idea, then breezily asked, "How goes it? Regards, Barry."

Female Interpretation: "I hope he really doesn't expect a response to his silly question about how life is going for me. Why did he even bother to ask? Did he show he was even remotely interested in finding out about me, and who I am, and what I do?" Now she was starting to lose patience with a guy who apparently just wanted to gab about superficial things in the news.

Leila did not hear from Barry again for days. So she initiated an email, keeping her tone similar to his: "Hi, Barry, Interesting idea you have. Let's talk about it on the phone or on Saturday night. Speaking of Saturday night, please tell me where you want to go. Since you don't know my neighborhood, would you like me to make reservations somewhere?"

Two days later, Barry called. They made definite plans about where they would meet, which was at the hotel at which he was staying, but he never said anything about the kind of food he likes or the kind of restaurant he preferred. Leila assumed they would eat at the hotel. Surprisingly, this hotel was in her immediate vicinity, a suburb of the city.

Female Interpretation: "This guy said he needed to do business in the city. So why is he staying in this suburb near my town?"

Leila didn't ask him about his true intentions, because she thought that might embarrass him. (This is another example of how women, unlike men, try to protect others' feelings, often at the price of their own.) But Leila figured she'd get the lowdown the night of their date.

Already, this guy was a mystery. All it seemed

he wanted to do was to talk politics and discuss stories in the news. Why did he want to drive south two hours to have the same discussion they could have online or on the phone?

The First Date

Leila met Barry at his hotel lobby. When he looked at her, he said he remembered her as having auburn hair, when, in reality, she had blonde.

Female Interpretation: "What exactly *did* he remember about me that entranced him that night? If he didn't even remember my hair color, and he wasn't interested in getting to know me, what does he want?"

Since they had no dinner reservations, Leila suggested they find a quiet restaurant where they could talk. The hotel's reservations for dinner were totally booked. This was poor planning on Barry's part, since he knew he was staying there, and he might have made reservations at the hotel for dinner when he booked his room. Actually, it was he who had mentioned to Leila that they might want to eat at the hotel weeks earlier over the phone.

It was pouring, so the pair wanted to do little traveling to stay dry. But that didn't happen. They drove to something hopefully nearby, and found an overly lit Mexican restaurant, which was too crowded. They tried a local pub, which was too noisy. Finally, they had no choice but to settle into a restaurant /pizzeria, hardly a place a guy would want to take a lady to make a good first impression. But it was quiet and dry, and after traveling aimlessly for an hour with no success, Leila had enough.

Female Interpretation: "If this dude had had the brains to respond to my email about making reservations, this endless traveling in the pouring rain could have been avoided."

The duo settled at a table and talked for hours. In fact, the waitress had to ask them to settle their check, so the restaurant could finally close. Leila discovered that Barry had three daughters. He didn't ask her out for the week immediately following the gala, he said, because he was with his kids. She asked why he hadn't revealed that up front. He said he didn't want her to think he was an overly devoted father.

Female Interpretation: "This guy is very shy and socially clumsy."

But the fact that he cared deeply for his daughters was appealing. Then he finally revealed that seeing Leila this Saturday night was the *only* reason he had driven the two hours near her town.

Female Interpretation: "This guy is obviously crazy about me: He drove this distance in this horrible weather, he tried to conceal his parental status, and he worked very hard to impress me. If he only knew that planning for a dinner reservation would have impressed me more!"

Barry's story was that now he had a divorce and a rebound relationship behind him by a few years. He also seemed anxious to establish a lasting romance. When they returned to his hotel after midnight, he asked her to come in. She politely refused, but their first kiss told of more to come. Barry invited Leila to return in the morning to join him at the hotel for brunch.

Female Interpretation: "Yesss!"

Leila slept well that night. When she got to Barry's hotel room on Sunday morning, the couple couldn't keep their lips and hands off each other. Brunch lasted another six hours, as the couple spoke at length about their jobs, life, Barry's daughters, their goals, and their families. At that point, Leila was glad she hadn't closed the door on Barry's clumsy courtship. But she had to leave for a party in the city. When they said goodbye, Barry told her he was thrilled about the time they spent together. She said that she was elated, too.

The Follow-Up

The following Monday morning, Leila got this cheery message from the new man in her life: "Good morning, Leila, there's sunshine here and I'm about to begin my day. Attached are the web sites I told you about that you had asked for, and I'll send more later. Regards . . . no, make that Love ya, Barry."

Female Interpretation: "Love ya!" "Hmmm . . . This guy definitely wants a relationship."

As promised, Barry sent the additional info later with this greeting: "Hi, Leila, The information you asked for is attached. How is it going today? Toodledoo, Barry."

Leila responded with a brief note describing her last couple of days. It was short, informative, and upbeat.

A few days elapsed. There was no phone call from Barry, but then came an impersonal email, whose Subject was, "This is right up your alley" and it was a lead for Leila's business.

Female Interpretation: "How nice that I'm on Barry's mind even during his chaotic work life."

Although this email didn't expand the warmth of his earlier "love ya," she chalked it up to his busy schedule, with a hope of more to come. This is so typical of women, who forever try to analyze reasons for a guy's behavior.

Sure enough, that night she got another email: "Hi Leila, I've been having problems with my home computer, and . . . He proceeded to say he was sorry for not contacting her sooner. How are you doing?? Barry."

Friday's email was more emotionally promising, Leila thought, because Barry included the "love ya" closing again: "Hi, Leila, Thought you'd be interested in the attached information. Love ya, Barry."

It was nice that when Barry saw information that might benefit Leila, he'd send it to her. She didn't hear from him all weekend, but she figured he was busy playing Daddy. She assumed, and hoped, she would see him the following weekend.

On the Tuesday following the weekend, she received another "Hi, Leila . . ." It went on, "This article looks like something you'd be interested in. Love ya, Barry." Attached was a 9-page document. There was nothing personal. That was it.

Female Interpretation: "Well, he's still emotionally keyed in. I can't wait to hear what he has to say on the telephone when he calls, about when we can see each other again."

That same evening, she got this: "Hi, Sweet Leila, hope you're well. We're having a very busy week at my office already, and it's still only Tuesday. Did you catch the article in the paper I sent you about the Ebola virus? The political climate here is very tense now. Love ya, Barry."

After exchanging numerous emails with the same general non-personal tone, Barry called Leila on Wednesday to chat. They remained on the phone for an hour and a half, getting to know more about each other.

Female Interpretation: "Great communication! Most men hate talking on the phone, except to get facts or make plans. ("REPORT" talk!) Speaking to me for so long is a great sign."

Leila even fantasized that Barry knew this:

Gilda-Gram®

The way to a woman's heart is not between her legs; it's between her ears.

Maybe this guy had more on the ball than Leila originally thought! Or, maybe she was just telling herself what she was hoping would be the case.

When they next spoke, Leila told Barry that while his emails were very thoughtful, she felt the phone was much more intimate. He said he wanted to visit her over the weekend, and could probably be there on Saturday at about 6PM. She graciously said he didn't have to incur the expense of a hotel room again, and invited him to stay with her. She never said she only had one bed, which necessitated their sleeping side by side. But, with all the smooching they had done two weeks earlier, she didn't think that would be a problem.

Dated Friday at 1AM, Barry sent Leila another email, this being the most intimate ever: "Hello, sweet one . . . The hour is late, so I won't call and disturb your sleep. But I thought I'd just click one off to you, as you presumably slumber in the gentle darkness . . . It was a long day with all the news." (He then continued on with three paragraphs of political news.) Then, "Love ya . . . Miss ya . . . Barry."

Female Interpretation: "What a tender note to wake up to! I can't wait to have this guy next to me in my bed this weekend."

That Saturday morning, she received another email: "Hi, Leila, I know you hate these emails . . ."

Female Interpretation: "I never said that! All I told him was that I like the sound of his voice *better* than the sight of his words. I never said I hated his emails."

Barry continued, "But since this one is about a

web address that would be helpful to your business, I
thought I'd click it off to you. Love ya, Barry."

And then, at 6:30PM, he was there.
Disappointingly, there was no "sweep-her-off-her-feet"
hello kiss. Instead, after the two-hour drive, he rushed
into her apartment sweating profusely, he gave her a
peck on the cheek, and he ran to where nature called
him, something he said he had been putting off for the
last hour. Nonetheless, Leila was delighted he was
there.

When Barry emerged from the bathroom, Leila
showed him around. They plunked down on the sofa,
where Leila offered him some wine, but which he
refused. He suggested they grab a bite to eat.

The couple headed to one of the local places to
just sit and talk. Intellectually, Barry captivated her
attention. Emotionally, she thought she could begin to
fall.

After they returned from the restaurant, in her
dimly lit living room, the couple sipped the leftover
wine, while soft music mellowed the mood. Barry
moved from the chair opposite Leila onto the sofa beside
her. They kissed gently, and he held her tight. On the
way into the bedroom, they stopped in her office, where
he showed her another beneficial web site.

Leila felt a void being filled that she hadn't even known had been empty. How wonderful to receive such caring from someone who genuinely wanted to help her. When the couple finally did end up in bed, Leila felt a new bond. They made love and delightfully fell asleep.

Morning came and Leila wanted to extend the night's closeness, and lounge around in bed. They made love again, and fell asleep for a brief time. But without warning, Barry loudly BOLTED out of bed, saying he wanted to head back home. Leila was flabbergasted. She had assumed that, like the last time he had driven to see her, they would grab brunch and spend the day together.

But Barry was in an unmistakable hurry. He asked for directions for a place to get coffee. On his way out the door, he was carrying his overnight satchel. Almost sarcastically, she asked if he intended to return with coffee and bagels for the two of them. He laughed, embarrassed, and said of course, but it would save time to put his things in the trunk now. It was obvious that he couldn't get out of Leila's house soon enough!

<u>Female Interpretation</u>: "Oh, puleese! Here is another guy who fears closeness and intimacy! Take your leave, sucker!"

Barry hadn't showered, shaved, or brushed his teeth, but he was walking out with all his toiletries. Independent Leila savored the time alone to pretty herself up for the rest of the day. Barry had said he'd return, but she wasn't counting on it.

Half an hour later, the two of them were eating in Leila's kitchen. Barry then began to complain about all the things he had to do that day. As she listened, she became turned off. She told him that she had refused an invitation for Sunday brunch because she assumed the two of them would be together. He said he now felt guilty. Obviously, he wasn't feeling guilty enough to alter his intentions. But as much of a hurry as he said he was in, he continued to hang around with Leila for another two hours. "More B.S.," Leila thought. Finally, he kissed her goodbye, without even asking how she planned to spend the rest of her day.

Female Interpretation: "Ohhh! This guy is screwed up. Who needs this?"

When she awoke Monday morning, there was an email from Barry, as though nothing unusual had occurred on Sunday: "Hi, Hon, check out this web site. It has a menu of all the yacht clubs in our state, as we were discussing. Love ya, Barry."

Female Interpretation: "What? OK, maybe I was too quick to judge Barry. Maybe he was just frightened by his own feelings. Maybe he needs time."

Leila wisely knew:

Gilda-Gram®

A woman can't hurry a guy into love.

But like most women, she took the hit for judging too soon, misreading this dude, and disregarding Barry's precious feelings.

So as not to make herself crazy, Leila chose to go about her business, deciding to see what would happen next, without falling into any more typical female overanalyzing of Barry's behavior.

The following day, she took the lead by forwarding Barry an article she thought he's like. She didn't hear a response throughout the entire week. Finally, late Sunday night, after he presumably was with his kids, she got a lengthy email of a script he had written that day to accompany a documentary he had produced. His salutation began: "Hi again, Dear One," and ended with the usual "Love ya, Barry."

Moments later, a much warmer email arrived. "Hello, Dear One, just a quick note while this is on my mind. Tomorrow there will be a show about women in business that you might find interesting. I went for a walk tonight, and hopefully will build up to the point where I can run without expiring on the sidewalk (gasp, gasp). I am getting a little gut and have to work on turning my droopy tummy into a Tarzan washboard (though that jut jaw of mine will always be mistaken for

Cheetah's)."

That note made Leila smile. However, it also got her to see Barry in another light.

<u>Female Interpretation</u>: "I can't believe this handsome hunk lacks a positive image of himself!"

Barry's email continued, "The kids and I had a fun softball game today, but it amazes me how many parents just sit on their ample bottoms, and do nothing to assist those of us who are volunteering to make it happen. These parents just drive up, drop the kids off, and leave. They obviously view us—strangers—as their babysitters. I hope you can accomplish everything you started. You are amazing! Love ya, Barry."

<u>Female Interpretation</u>: "Does he mean he hopes I accomplish all the things I started *in my life*? That's the problem with words that are written instead of spoken on the phone or in person. Maybe this is a kiss-off. I haven't gotten a phone call from him since he escaped my 'prison.' While they're entertaining, these emails are not enough to sustain a relationship, at least with me. Yet, they appear to be sufficient for Barry. Maybe he's just lonely, and wants a buddy with whom he can share political news. If that's the case, See Ya!"

Leila found herself becoming more and more fed up. With still no word from Barry by phone, she called him the following night. All he wanted to do was talk politics. He mentioned that he might visit her the following weekend. She wondered whether that was his real intention, or whether it was a face-saving line.

Female Interpretation: "*Might* visit me? What am I? A nomad's inn? Besides, he didn't even bother to ask if I were available! Yet, I like the idea of seeing him again. So I'll just ignore my gut feelings."

Leila had also allowed herself to let down her protective guard. By the time Thursday rolled around, there was still no word from Barry about whether he intended to drive down to see her.

Female Interpretation: "Keeping me hanging like this is disrespectful. Now I'm really pissed off."

When she hadn't heard from him by Friday afternoon, she called him. He apologetically told her he was very tired from working night and day, and he wasn't coming. He said it was a long trip from his house to hers.

Female Interpretation: "Duh! No shit, Sherlock! Was this a sudden revelation? I'm well aware of the two-hour distance between us."

And then he suddenly lunged into a litany of

complaints: he had gotten a speeding ticket on his way home from her house two weeks ago; he had been emotionally and sexually exhausted after they had been together; he needed a few weeks to be alone to straighten out his home that was in a shambles from his not being there (for one day!). But the best, or worst, whining complaint of all was that he just wanted to do "light dating" for now.

Female Interpretation: "This guy's nuts. I'm outta here!"

The Reality Check

After not being able to wait to see her, after concocting false pretenses of needing to do business in her city, after voicing enormous happiness about meeting her, and THEN bolting out her door the morning after, rarely calling on the phone, yet sending political and professional emails signed with "love ya's" and "miss ya's, Leila decided that Barry was probably less exhausted from seeing her than she was from his mixed messages!

Not going to allow this jerk to get away with treating her so poorly, she confronted him about all his disrespectful behavior. Sheepishly, he said he agreed with everything she said. He admitted to being self-absorbed. Another great revelation!

Female Interpretation: "Oh, who cares already? I'm so

over this—and him!'"

Leila told Barry that the coming week she had to travel to the Midwest on business. He said he would try to call her before she left. Already apathetic, she offered no response. He quickly changed the words "*try to call*" to "I *will* call you before you leave." She deleted his telephone number from her cell phone, so she wouldn't be tempted in a moment of loneliness to ever call him again.

Barry did call Leila the night before the morning of her departure. She was at a dinner and did not get the message until it was too late to return his call. But in the morning, before she left, she sent him an email, heading the Subject "Good-bye": "Barry, I rolled in too late last night, and I no longer have your phone number programmed into my cell phone, so I couldn't return your call from the road. I thought about you when I was meeting with other TV producers discussing documentaries they are writing. Have a good weekend. Leila."

Her note was friendly enough, but obviously impersonal. Perhaps they'd run into each other again at another big function some day. But it was clear that she was ready to continue her life without him.

Unlike anything he had ever done before with her, he wrote back *immediately*. She noticed the Subject on his email was changed from "Goodbye" to "Hello": "Hi, Leila, thanks for the note, though when I saw the Subject it knocked me out."

<u>Female Interpretation</u>: "Buddy, not as much as your mixed messages knocked *me* out!"

He continued, "I hope your trip is successful, and that you get some time to relax. It's been crazy at work, and I'll be traveling during the next two weeks covering the brewing political debates. Love ya, Barry."

<u>The End</u>

      This time, Leila didn't give Barry's empty "Love ya" another thought. His empty expressions were old and tired now. And she had no intention of revisiting this scene with this dude.

Gilda-Gram®

Despite what he tells you,
only his *behavior* tells the truth.

      Barry's behavior didn't support his words, and Leila had no interest in a long distance relationship, especially with a guy who was emotionally absent. As she reviewed the last couple of weeks, she recalled how

Barry described his ex-wife as "having a screw loose." She remembered he had also depicted his ex-girlfriend with "a screw loose." Based on her own experience with him, she now knew who it was that had a few loose screws.

Leila reviewed their lovemaking that had so "exhausted" him. She remembered he said that while he and his wife were divorcing, he didn't have sex for six months. He said the reason was because he was still legally married, and that went against his morality. Initially, Leila sized him up as very ethical.

Now, in retrospect, she saw him as a guy with a very low sex drive. At first, like most women, she wondered if she had been a good enough lover to satisfy him. But now she reviewed the facts with fresh eyes. A relationship just starting is usually heatedly sexy. From the get go, theirs was less than lukewarm.

Looking back, Leila had given the potential romance every opportunity to succeed. Her gut had told her to beware, but like many women, she chose to ignore the warnings. Barry's words *said* he wanted to get close and carnal, but he *showed* that he was only devoted to his job, his politics, and his kids—and probably in that order. She didn't care to analyze his problems further. When she pulled the plug, it was not a moment too soon.

If you're a woman reading this, did any part of it resonate with you? Everyone could save herself from relationship grief if she would only trust her gut's message to interpret the cues for what they are. Ignore the empty words you want to believe, and trust only the behavior being demonstrated. Your payoff is that you'd rid the people who drain you, and become more available for those who appreciate you—and deserve you.

PostScript

Barry had a big, prestigious job in the media, so when he did something noteworthy, it would make some headlines. One sleepy morning, Leila came across a column about how the News Director of Barry's News Channel had been found drunk, and slumped over in his car seat, having been there during the entire frigid night. Ordinarily, this kind of news item would not have attracted Leila's attention. But something told her to continue reading. It was a good thing she did, because when the report mentioned the name of the News Director, it was Barry!

"OMG!," thought Leila. "A drinking problem might explain this guy's crazy behavior and mixed messages." She sat there, staring at the story. Suddenly, she was very thankful she had glided out of the relationship before she had gotten any more involved.

Ultimately, Leila had criticized herself for not trusting her gut. But when her gut screamed so loudly, she had no choice but to pay attention. Guts always know best!! How many times have you ignored the messages sent to you by yours? And in the end, how did your own postscript turn out?

I know I often ended up proverbially kicking myself for not having heeded obvious warnings screaming at me at multiple times. Yet, that's how we learn. At some point, however, most of us agree we've had enough learning already, and that's when we finally choose to take better care of ourselves in our next encounters.

TIP #5

BELIEVE ONLY *CONSISTENT* BEHAVIOR

An earlier **Gilda-Gram®** said, "Despite what he tells you, only his behavior tells the truth." The problem is that when we're involved in relationships, we observe a lot of different behaviors. How do we determine which ones count as truth?

Dear Dr. Gilda,

I am 29 and have been in a weird relationship for over a year. I met Steve when we worked together, before I was transferred out of the company. There was electricity between us, but we were each attached elsewhere.

Months after not speaking, we met again at a nightclub. From then on, we took turns calling each other every night at 1AM, but not going out. He had just ended his 2-year relationship, and I was out of mine. Months later, we bumped into each other again. This time we kissed for the first time. I later asked what he thought of me, and he said that after his long and painful relationship, he didn't want anything serious right now. So I let it slide and we continued talking on the phone.

We met up with each other again at a nightclub for the third time and we kissed again. After that, for some reason, he refused to return my calls. I was in agony because I didn't know what I did wrong. Each day, I thought about him and hurt. I finally had my best friend call him, and ask why he stopped talking to me. He said he was angry because when his friend told me he was in the hospital, I laughed. He ended up being very sick.

A month later, he called to say that despite his anger, he still had feelings for me. We continued to talk on the phone, kiss at nightclubs, and he said he cared for me. Yet, he never asked me out! When I asked again what I meant to him, he said, "Why are you rushing this?" So I gave him still more time.

We continued to bump into each other at nightclubs, and sometimes even make out. I wrote him a 4-page letter describing my feelings. After reading it, he finally did ask me out. But now I was angry at him because one night while he was drunk, he tried to pull down my tube top. I refused to talk to him for a month. He called me from time to time to ask how I was doing, but I still harbored embarrassment and pain.

Finally, tired of wondering what I meant to him,

I called and asked him where we stood. He reiterated that he didn't want a girlfriend at this time. He also said I had some nerve not to talk to him for a month and then ask him that question.

Later that year, it all began again: we'd bump into each other at a nightclub and make out. This time, he wouldn't call me for a week at a time, and the conversations would be brief. Then we would hook up again at a nightclub. This is getting on my nerves and I don't know what to think anymore. Is he playing mind games with me?
Ellie

Steve *said* he was not ready for a girlfriend, yet he stayed on the phone with Ellie long into the night, knowing she cared for him. They even made out in front of their friends. But was Ellie an innocent bystander—and this story's victim?

Dear Ellie:
The first part of your email sounds like you care for a vulnerable man who needs time to heal after his breakup. You clearly heard what he told you and you agreed to wait. But then you became impatient, accusing him of mind games. It's true, he's sending mixed messages in saying he's not ready for romance, yet participating in this flirtation.

What I don't understand is your willingness to

play this game. If a guy isn't ready, he isn't ready.
Having a makeout session with you won't make him
more ready for love.

Gilda-Gram®

Men separate sex from love.
Women believe sex IS love.

Steve has repeatedly told you he doesn't want to
get serious now, and his behavior supports his words.
Are you so self-involved to think that you can change his
mind?

Your pushiness is not only creating permanent
damage for anything that might be possible in the future,
but it may also be slowing Steve's healing. You continue
to offer him sex (Yes, making out is sex), and you
continue to ask him where you stand. It upsets you that
he hasn't come around despite your seductiveness. You
want to know he cares for you, yet, if you had his
feelings at heart, you would follow his wishes.

How Steve treated you with your tank top is a
blaring sign about where you stand, which is, sorry to
say, nowhere. A man who cares for a woman doesn't
disrespect her with drunkenness and foul play. You
thought that by showing your anger, you'd manipulate

him into your heart.

He's right that you had some nerve not to talk to him and then to ask again where you stood. And you say that he's the one playing games?

Get real! Steve is not interested in you as you'd like him to be. If you aren't happy with the arrangement, find someone else. But if you continue to play similar games with a new guy, he will leave skid marks.

For now, you and Steve need a breather. Let him go and grow. Maybe someday, the two of you will meet again, ready for romance. But for now, it's just electricity without the necessary sparks.
Dr. Gilda

Especially since their attraction was great, Ellie refused to believe that Steve was not going to make himself available to her. People perceive, and then act on, circumstances through what we call "selective perception."

Gilda-Gram®
Our selective perception honors what we want to believe.

While Steve *said* he didn't want to rush a

relationship with Ellie, she chose to read his *behavior* of late-night phone calls and makeout sessions as a positive sign. Sure, behavior speaks louder than words. However, these behaviors were not the *right* behaviors for what Ellie wanted.

So how can you tell if the behaviors you perceive are the behaviors to believe?

Gilda-Gram®
**The only behaviors to trust
are those that continue over time.**

Over the course of time that Ellie knew Steve, there was no consistent display of affection. What was displayed was Steve's neediness for companionship, esteem-boosting, and female attention. Ellie wanted a man who cared. For now, it wasn't Steve.

If you are questioning whether certain behaviors are either too good to be true, or whether they truly reflect who your partner is, s-l-o-w down. Here's the rule to follow:

Gilda-Gram®
When in doubt, wait it out, and DO WITHOUT.

Over time, your answer will become obvious, even to you, who might want your story to end in a different way. Then it will be up to you to trust what you actually see—and to make do with that. Even if a story doesn't end happily-ever-after in a way that you might hope, recognize that there's something far better for you waiting somewhere else!

All you must do is tell the universe that you refuse to accept crumbs. After you are clear about that, you'll have the empty space to fill with a partner that's far more appropriate for your needs.

TIP #6

ASK FOR EXACTLY WHAT YOU WANT

Why don't men and women level with each other? Whether you're going out on a first date, or meeting a business associate for the first time, everyone wants to make a good initial impression. But having Toastmaster traits, women in particular want the people around them to be happy and like them. To make sure that happens, they will often withhold their desires, so that others are not inconvenienced, or so these women won't get rejected in their requests. The price people pay for this emotional "dishonesty" about what they truly want creates relationship disappointment.

Marty and Carol were newlyweds, living in their first apartment. One Sunday, Carol had set up a fun day of shopping with her best girlfriend. Marty's plan was to watch the football game on TV. Before she left on her excursion, while Marty was still asleep, Carol left him the following note: "Darling, if you get bored sometime during the day, please go to the hardware store and pick up eight screws for the screen door, like the

screw I'm leaving on this counter top. Love, Carol."
What Carol really meant was, "I want you to go to the
hardware store to get these eight lousy screws you
promised to get last week. It's important that you fix the
screen door, instead of spending the day like a couch
potato, watching your stupid football game." A little
hidden anger there? You bet!

When Carol returned from her fun day away, she
asked Marty if he had gotten the screws. He told her he
had spent the day indoors, enjoying the game. Instead of
being happy that Marty was finally relaxing from his
hectic job, Carol again tried to conceal her
disappointment. She knew she had not been totally
forthright about wanting Marty to fix the screen door
today. And besides, she felt a pang of guilt for enjoying
the day with her friend, while her new husband was left
to fend for himself on a beautiful Sunday.

Also, if she had asked Marty to get dressed and
go out, he might have suggested that since she would
already be out of the house, *she* should buy the screws
herself. At the base of it all, deeply hidden from
consciousness, Carol grew up in a household with a
father who often rejected her requests. So now, as
irrational as it would appear, she unconsciously feared
that Marty would automatically reject her wishes, also.

As much as she tried to hide it, Carol's
disappointment showed. Her husband had no idea why
she came home so upset from a fun day with her best

girlfriend. He asked if she and her friend had had a fight. He wanted to know if he had done something to irritate her. He asked if she was suffering from PMS. When she said no to all his questions, he decided to let it rest, and continued to watch TV, which further annoyed Carol. Have you, or any of your female friends, found yourself in a similar situation?

Expressing our true wants requires us to deal with many more elements than appear on the surface:

Gilda-Gram®

Our willingness to make requests reflects our childhood experiences, our self-esteem, and our security in our relationship.

If a woman is stuck in Toastmaster mode, she must come face-to-face with these issues. Since her man hears information best as a factual "report, " if she speaks in his language, she has a greater chance of being heard.

Carol needed to level with herself about what prevented her from being totally honest with her husband. Then, all she had to say was, "Honey, we still need those eight screws, so you can fix the screen door. If I were going to be near the store, I'd buy them myself. I feel guilty even asking you to pull yourself away from your game. But if you don't do this today, you won't be able to get to this job until next weekend, and a big storm is predicted for tomorrow." This way, she would have been sharing her feelings, letting him know why she herself wasn't buying the screws, and communicating the urgency of her request. How could her husband possibly have refused her then?

Issuing honest messages makes us feel stronger in the relationship and also cuts down on misunderstanding. Sure, sometimes the people we love disappoint us. But if that occurs, communicate your disappointment. When the screws were not there when Carol returned, she might have said, "I'm disappointed you didn't buy the screws today." Then the issue would have been done with, over and out! In this way, Carol would have gotten her upset off her chest, and Marty would not have been left to wonder why she was out of whack.

If honest communication is not part of your relationship from the start, the dishonesty will build over time, and lead to a breakdown of your entire relationship. This dysfunction is easy to nip in the bud!!

TIP #7:

ADMIT YOUR ANGER

Getting angry is as common as getting the common cold. But contrary to what most people think, it's actually a good emotion, because it lets you know that circumstances are not right, and something needs to be done to change them.

Women think they are better communicators than men, because they are so intuitive. But they have a tough time expressing their anger. An angry woman says, "I am upset," or "frustrated," or "confused," or "hurt," but she rarely admits that she is "angry." This is because admitting to being angry destroys the image of the "good girl" accommodator that little girls are taught to be.

So because women tend to bury their anger rather than express it, I find myself needing to read between the lines of much of the email and in-person dialogues I get from women. That's the only way I can understand the real emotions beneath the words.

Dear Dr. Gilda,

I spent a year of my life in a relationship with a man I adored. He was the best thing that ever happened to me. But at the time, I treated him horribly. I had been in three bad relationships before him, and I admit I took all my frustrations out on him. When he finally broke up with me, I thought I was going to die. But then, months later, he returned to my life and wanted me back.

At the time, I was already dating someone else. But we got back together for two weeks, and I thought everything was great. However, when I discovered he was also dating someone else, I asked him to show me respect by breaking up with her. After the two weeks, he told me he didn't love me as he used to, because of all the pain I had put him through. I insisted I am better now, and I begged him to stay, so we could work things out. He left anyway, and now I'm alone and heartbroken.
Jessie

Dear Jessie,

Let's get real here: More than "heartbroken," you're ANGRY! 1) You are angry with yourself for getting involved in three dysfunctional relationships, one after another. 2) You are angry with yourself for mistreating this guy you were crazy about. 3) You are angry with yourself for not dealing with your anger, and for allowing yourself to blow your stack—with the wrong person! 4) You are angry with this guy because, despite your pleas for him to leave his new woman, he rejected your wishes.

Anger should never be buried. If it is, it won't just lie dormant. It will either do damage to your body in the form of stress that causes disease, or it will stay inside you until it blows—at the wrong time, at the wrong place, with the wrong person. Because women have such difficulty admitting their anger, it may be the most misdirected emotion they have.

Gilda-Gram®
**Don't act anger in, or act anger out.
Act anger *through*.**

Acting anger through involves acknowledging it, and accepting its real sources. Since you "adored" this guy, you could have brought him closer, by honestly sharing your emotions. This doesn't mean singing a "poor-me, look-what-these-guys-before-you-did-to-me" song. No! By just letting him know that you were hurting, and asking for his patience and support, you would have been communicating your vulnerability. Contrary to what most women believe,

Gilda-Gram®
Vulnerability isn't weakness; it's humanness.

Vulnerability draws people closer. Relationships are in our life to teach us not about our partner, but about ourselves. Jessie, you learned a valuable lesson.

I'm sorry your romance didn't have a happy ending, but from now on, you'll be able to steer your next relationships in a different and healthier direction. All you can do now is be grateful for your new knowledge and future growth.
Dr. Gilda

Knowledge becomes power only if we apply it. My friend, Barbara, was in the midst of an angry divorce, and she was very depressed.

Gilda-Gram®
Depression is anger turned inward.

Women tend to act anger *in*, while men tend to act anger *out*. These behaviors are supported by our society that names women as pleasantly "passive," and men as successfully "aggressive."

Barbara decided to visit New York for a week to try to reestablish former business ties. A man she barely knew enticed her to stay at his house in a remote suburb of Connecticut, by promising to drive her into Manhattan each time she needed to get to meetings. She consented to the offer on a "friends-only" basis. Without a clue, she was too depressed and naïve to recognize that there are no free rides.

She met me for dinner one night. When her host later joined us, I was impressed with his good looks, and I was happy that Barbara had found at least a temporary diversion from her nasty husband. But during our conversation, I discovered that at 34, this guy had never had a woman in his life for more than a year—and that was only once. He claimed to have just sold his business to a large firm, but his explanations sounded sketchy.

While he talked, I saw he liked Barbara as more than a friend. I also found that before he completed one thought, he'd be on to the next. His dialogue was so disjointed, I had to ask him questions about what he had just said so the conversation could remain focused. This guy was obviously so fearful of commitment, he had trouble committing to a complete sentence! Yet, I could see that he was a heartbreaker, and I feared that my friend would now have to deal with another crushing disappointment, on top of her divorce.

When it was time for me to leave, I said my goodbyes, and promised Barbara we'd talk soon. I recognized that people in the midst of divorce are never quite in their right mind, including myself, during which time I had several car accidents. So when I returned to my car, I called Barbara's cell phone, warning her about jumping into a new relationship when she was still raging over her old one.

If you're in an angry state, instead of falling into

the usual female custom of acting anger *in*, or even the male custom of acting anger *out*, understand the need to act anger *through*. As difficult as it may seem, accept your anger for what it really is, discuss it with people who care about you, and allow it to guide you to dismantle the relationship pulling you down.

This is how to act anger *through* in a calm and fruitful way. If you learn this skill now, it will promote your health, your career, and the positive relationships that you're yet to attract.

TIP #8

ASSESS YOUR MOTIVES

Men have assumed the reputation for being "commitment-phobic," while women are usually pegged for pushing for more. Yet, every relationship consists of two people. While one partner may be more reluctant to withhold his feelings, if the other person agrees to remain with him, she shares some of the responsibility for the relationship's direction.

Dear Dr. Gilda,

I've been divorced for 5 years, with lots of dumb relationships in between. I am 42 years old, with two kids, 14 and 11. Last year at this time, I went to a motorcycle meet, and approached an attractive man. Actually, I later stood him up, and I don't even know why. But in May, I called him, we got together for a motorcycle open house, and we had a great time.

This guy is considerate, kind, loving, and we get along great with a lot in common. He has a Harley and so do I, and we enjoy the same things. We get to see each other every other weekend, when I don't have my kids. I told him I don't want to involve my children in any relationship we have, and he was fine with that. I miss him when I don't see him.

His philosophy about love is that as soon as things start getting serious, all the fun disappears. Because of my own experiences with past relationships, I believe he's right. I have been single for a year, and he has been, too. He has no kids, and he's never been married.

He is 37 years old. A neighbor describes him as "a woman in a man's body," because he is so compassionate. Everything is great between us, including the sex. He even makes me breakfast when I stay with him. The two weeks I go without seeing him, however, just kills me, and now I find I'm getting terribly depressed when he's not around.

He does make plans in advance with me, like with our bikes, lake parties, and other events. How can I handle the time I am away from him? I don't want him to see a negative side of me.

Although I realize that everyone has dark moments, I don't want to make mine obvious. How much time should I wait to let him know, "Hey, I really like you"? I'd also like to ask, "Are we in an exclusive relationship?"

*I do know that neither of us has seen anyone
since we've been dating. He even told me I could
answer the phone one day while I was waiting for a call
from my girlfriend after her surgery. He said he hasn't
had any girls call him for a long time. I have met his
friends, neighbors, and even his family. This is one
relationship I don't want to mess up. What should I do?
Betsy*

Betsy senses there is a commitment problem with
this guy. Yet, he shows up when he promises, he has
introduced her to his family and friends, and he is caring
and compassionate. So why does Betsy feel this way?

*Dear Betsy,
On the surface, this guy certainly sounds well
matched for you, but I believe he's even better matched
for you than you realize. At the motorcycle meet where
you met him, you were the pursuer. But as soon as he
showed interest and made a date with you, you stood
him up. You casually dismissed your behavior with, ". .
. I don't even know why."*

*When you recognized he was not breaking down
the door to pursue you after that, you called him. Now
that you've been involved for some time, you say his
philosophy of love is that as soon as things get close, the
spark goes out, and you agree with his take on
relationships. You have never included your two*

*teenagers in any of the festivities you enjoy with this guy,
although he has certainly added you to his social circle.
This is not to say that kids ought to be immersed in their
mom's dating scenes. But after this, wouldn't you want
them to meet your special friend?*

*Concealing the fact that you have a social life
sends your children the message that you are content
with a life without love. This man seems to be
everything you want in a mate, yet after a year, you still
have not questioned his exclusivity or even what he sees
as your future together. Why?*

*Just because he's never married and he has no
children doesn't necessarily make him a commitment-
phobe. Maybe he hasn't yet found someone he wants to
spend his life with. Maybe he's been waiting for the
right person, and it is you. While you sense that he fears
a relationship—and that may or may not be the case—
you must also look in the mirror to see that it is YOU
who fear commitment!*

Gilda-Gram®
We attract not whom we want, but who we are.

*By your own admission, between your divorce
five years ago, and the "dumb" relationships you've*

been involved in since, your love life hasn't been terrific. It would stand to reason that you would be reluctant to want to get hurt again. However, you're a grown woman and you know that without risks, there are no rewards.

So Betsy, are you afraid of asking your guy these probing questions, because you're fearful that he might be turned off? Or, are you really fearful that he might be turned ON, and want to take the romance to the next level, which terrifies you because of your own past?

Real relationships do expose our "negative side," but they also reflect the other wonderful traits that our lover already appreciates. If you are ready for a relationship, commitment and all, it's time to stop hanging out in Play-land. If this guy turns out to be commitment-phobic after all, understand that he will cut and run, as soon as you want to deepen your union. But finding that out now sure beats being depressed in this guy's absence.

Face the truth: you really no longer support your guy's philosophy of love, and it is just possible that he no longer supports it either. Your depression is telling you that you want more with this "warm and compassionate" man, and you see that it's unhealthy to conceal your emotions. Take the risk of suggesting that the two of you step-up the romance, and you just may finally reap the love you want. If not, you will never find out!

Dr. Gilda

It's always easier and more convenient to blame an alleged commitment-phobic man as the reason your relationship has not moved further along. However,

<u>Gilda-Gram®</u>

Each of us plays a role in every relationship in which we're involved.

Listen honestly to your internal voice. If it tells you that you want more than you're getting, follow your heart to pursue it. The worst thing that could happen is that you discover sooner rather than later that it's time to move to a more promising prospect. Do you have the guts to go with that possibility?

CONCLUSION

Your Future Is Up to You!

Male/female communication is not that difficult. It merely requires acknowledging our different language codes, and translating them into a dialect your partner can understand. The sooner you master the differences between our genders, and decode them using the above 8 Tips, the more solid your relationships will be—now and forever! Please let me know!!

***

**Benefit from
Dr. Gilda's personal Advice & Coaching
www.DrGilda.com**

***

MORE BOOKS BY DR. GILDA

Dr. Gilda's Relationship Series
--8 Steps to a Sizzling Marriage
--8 Tips to Understand the Opposite Sex

--10 Questions Single Women Should Never Ask
& 10 They Should
--10 Signs of a Cheater-to-Be

Dr. Gilda's Self-Worth Series
--I'm Worth Loving! Here's Why.
--Ask for What You Want—AND GET IT!
--How to Be a Worry-Free Woman

Dr. Gilda's Fidelity Series
--Why Your Cheater Keeps Cheating—And You're
Still There!
--How to Cope with the Cheater You Love—and WIN
--99 Prescriptions for Fidelity: *Your Rx for Trust*

ALSO
--Don't Bet on the Prince! *How to Have the Man You
Want by Betting on Yourself*
--Don't Lie on Your Back for a Guy Who Doesn't
Have Yours

***

Dr. Gilda Carle (Ph.D.) is an internationally
known media personality and relationship expert. She
has authored 15 books, including "Don't Bet on the
Prince!" (a test question on "Jeopardy!"), "Teen Talk
with Dr. Gilda," "He's Not All That! " "How to WIN
When Your Mate Cheats" (winner of The London Book
Festival literary award), "99 Prescriptions for Fidelity,"
and more. She also wrote the weekly "30-Second
Therapist" column for the Today Show, and the "Ask
Dr. Gilda" advice columnist for Match.com.

On TV, Dr. Gilda was the regular therapist for

the Sally Jessy Raphael show, the "Love Doc" for MTV Online, and the TV host of "The Dr. Gilda Show" pilot for Twentieth Century Fox. In addition, she was the therapist in HBO's Emmy Award winner, "Telling Nicholas," featured on Oprah, where she guided a family to tell their 7-year-old that his mom died in the World Trade Center bombing.

In the corporate sector and in academia, she has her own management consulting firm, she is Professor Emerita, and she is a motivational speaker and a product spokesperson for such brands as Harlequin Books, Hallmark Cards, Cottonelle, Galderma Pharmaceuticals, Match.com, and more.

As President of Country Cures, Inc., her non-profit 501(c)(3) educational charity, she is the "Country Music Doctor." The organization uniquely uses country music to re-build the relationships of re-entering veterans and their families. If you, or someone you know, can benefit from this help, please visit www.CountryCures.org.

Reach Dr. Gilda at
www.DrGilda.com
or
www.CountryCures.org

www.ingramcontent.com/pod-product-compliance
Lightning Source LLC
Chambersburg PA
CBHW071630040426
42452CB00009B/1568